בס"ד

לד׳ הארץ ומלואה

This book belongs to:

_____

Please read it to me!

Dedicated by Yosef Yitzchak & Penina Batsheva Popack
In honor of the birth of their daughter Sara Tivona,
and in honor of their other children,
Leah Eliana, Chana Tova, and Shayna Rivka.

The Waiting Wall

For my father, who hasn't been to the Kotel...yet. L.B.L.

First Edition - 5769 / 2009
Copyright © 2009 by HACHAI PUBLISHING
ALL RIGHTS RESERVED

Editor: D.L. Rosenfeld
Managing Editor: Yossi Leverton
Layout: Eli Chaikin

ISBN: 978-1-929628-49-0
LCCN: 2009927317

HACHAI PUBLISHING
Brooklyn, New York
Tel: 718-633-0100 Fax: 718-633-0103
www.hachai.com info@hachai.com

Printed in China

Glossary

Beis HaMikdosh . . . . . . The Holy Temple
Hashem . . . . G-d
Kosel HaMaarovi . . . . The Western Wall
Moshiach . . . . Messiah
Tefillah . . . . Prayer
Yerushalayim . . . . Jerusalem

Note

Many Jews refer to the Western Wall as the *Kosel*. Others use the pronunciation *Kotel*. Depending on the audience, either can be used when reading this story aloud.

The Waiting Wall

by Leah Braunstein Levy
illustrated by Avi Katz

Hachai
PUBLISHING

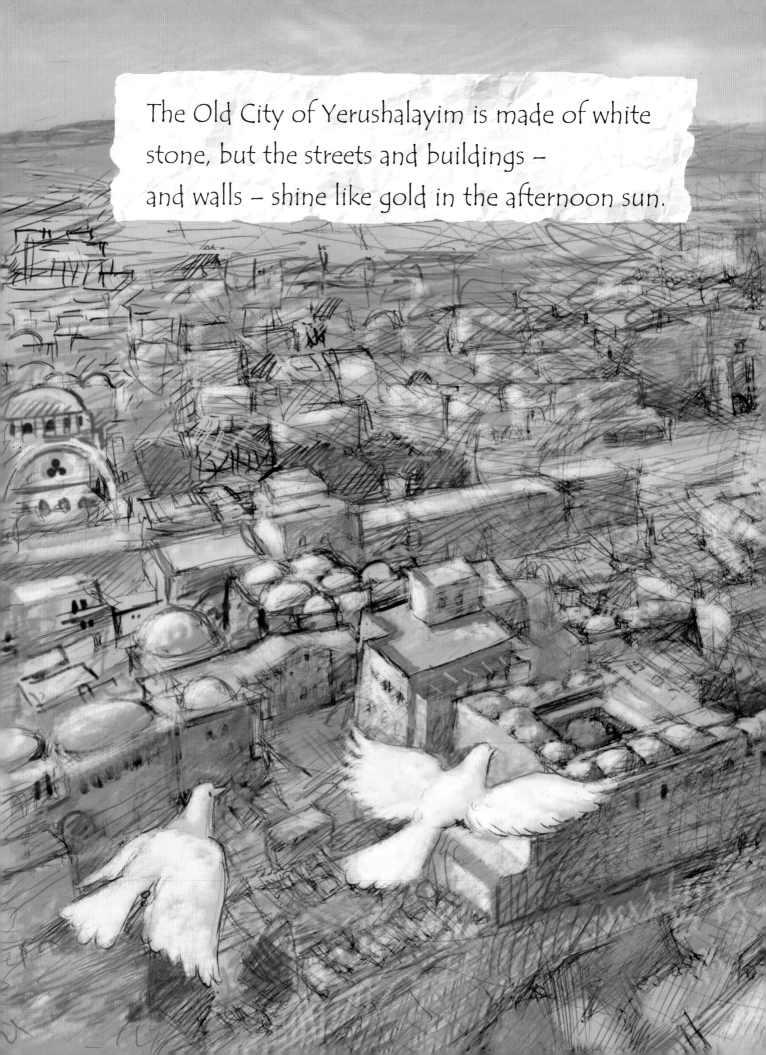

The Old City of Yerushalayim is made of white stone, but the streets and buildings – and walls – shine like gold in the afternoon sun.

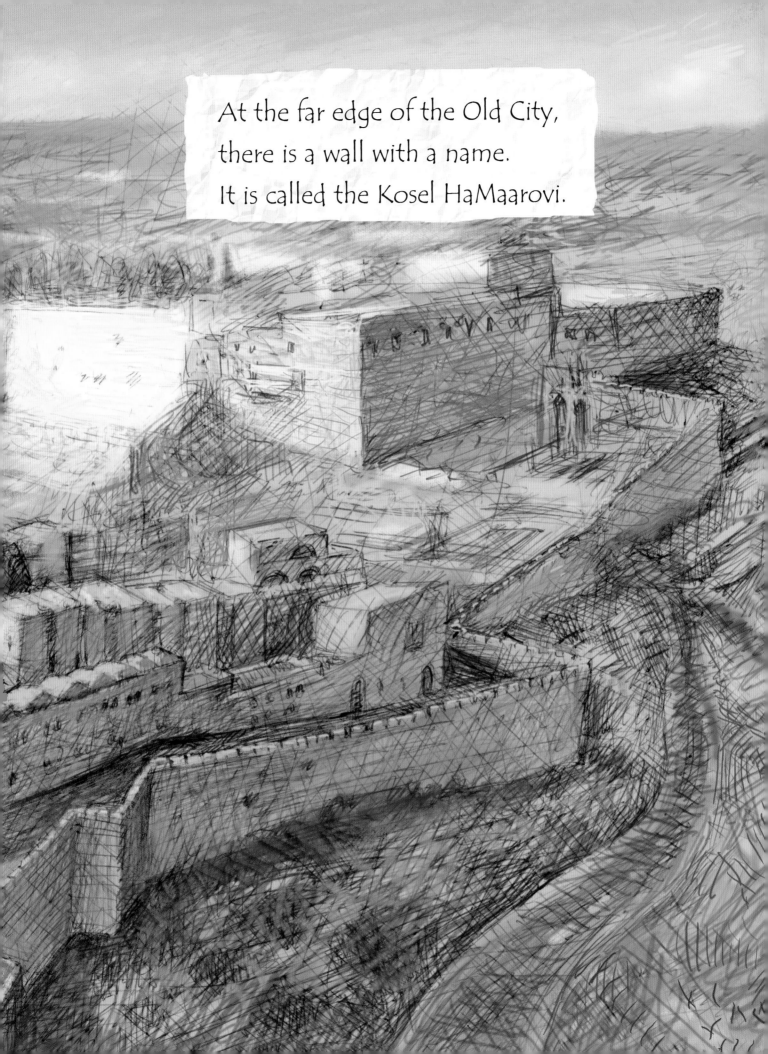

At the far edge of the Old City,
there is a wall with a name.
It is called the Kosel HaMaarovi.

When you go to the Kosel from inside the Old City, you walk down stairs, hundreds of stairs. Stop on the stairs and rest, look down, see what lies below.

You will see a wide empty space that stretches out to the Kosel. There are people walking around down there. From where you're standing, they look like colored shapes wandering on a wide, white floor.

The Kosel reaches arms across the shining empty space, holding it quiet and still.

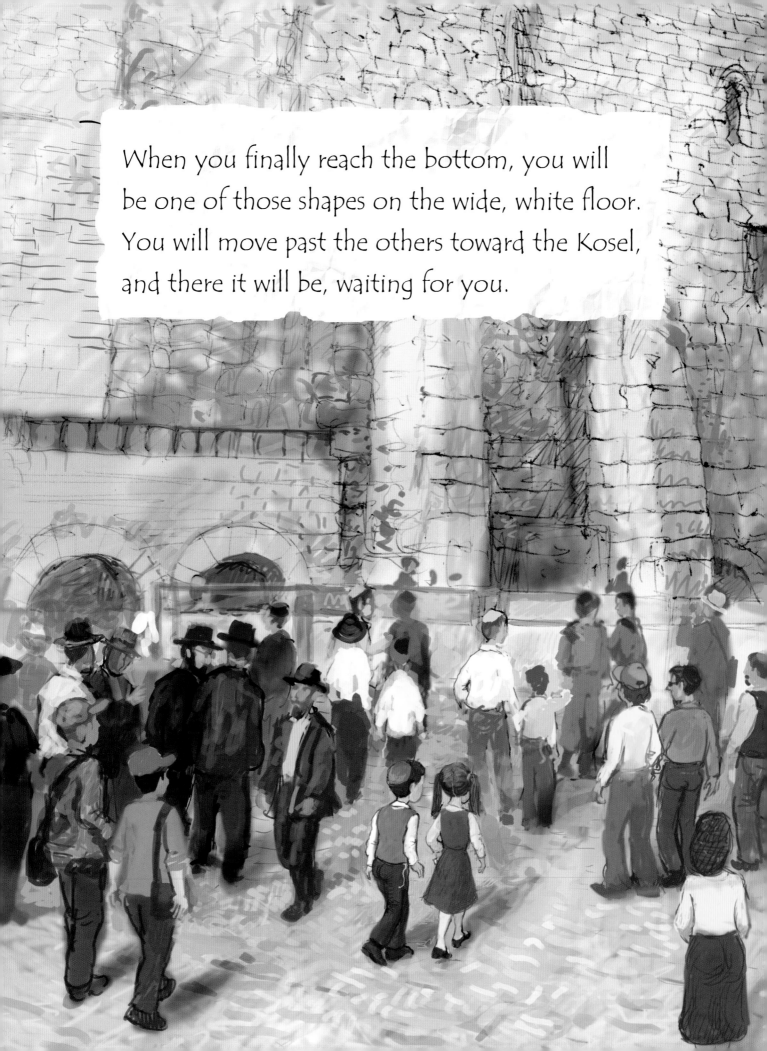

When you finally reach the bottom, you will be one of those shapes on the wide, white floor. You will move past the others toward the Kosel, and there it will be, waiting for you.

A very long time ago, the Beis HaMikdosh stood on the other side of the Kosel. The Beis HaMikdosh was a special place. Think of it as Hashem's home here on earth.

This is still His special place. It's easy to feel close to Hashem here. All around you, people bend and sway in tefillah like trees in the wind.

The Kosel is made of giant stones, each one as tall as you, reaching up to the blue, blue sky. The stones are older than you can imagine.

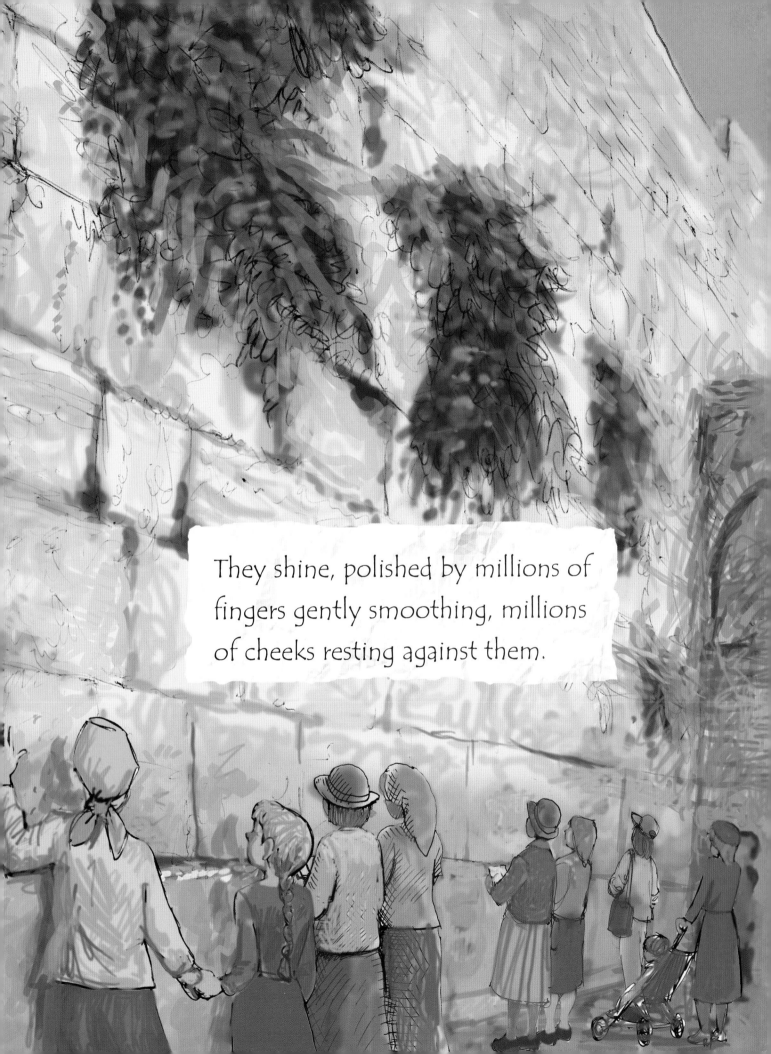

They shine, polished by millions of fingers gently smoothing, millions of cheeks resting against them.

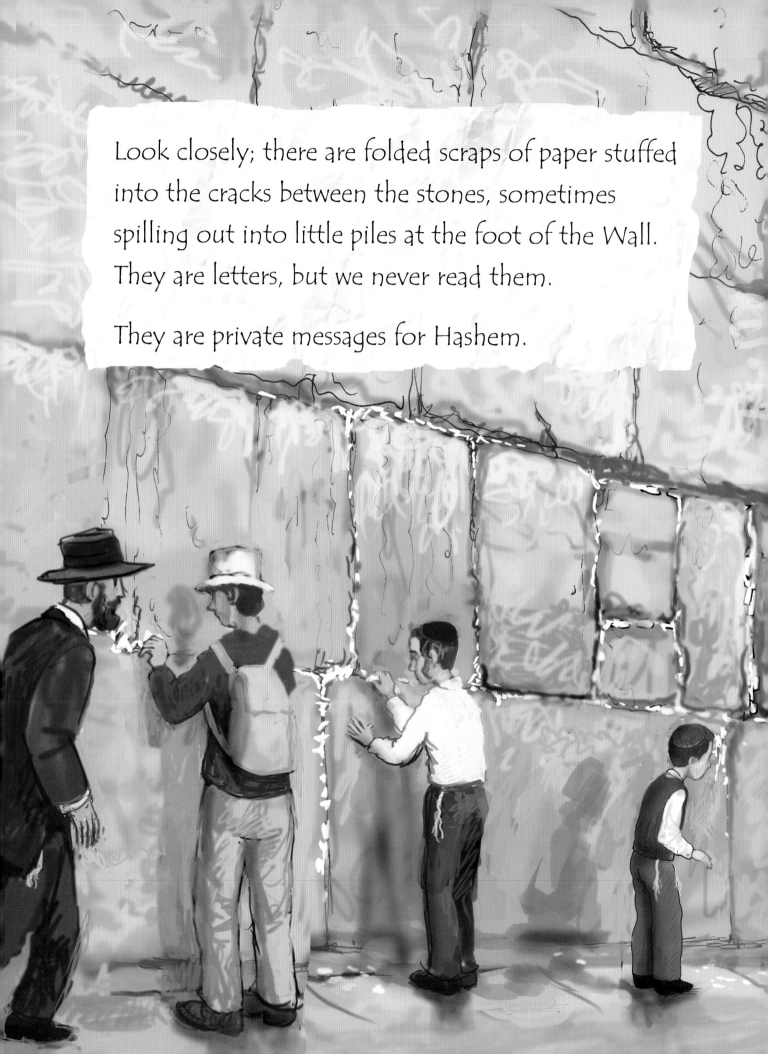

Look closely; there are folded scraps of paper stuffed into the cracks between the stones, sometimes spilling out into little piles at the foot of the Wall. They are letters, but we never read them.

They are private messages for Hashem.

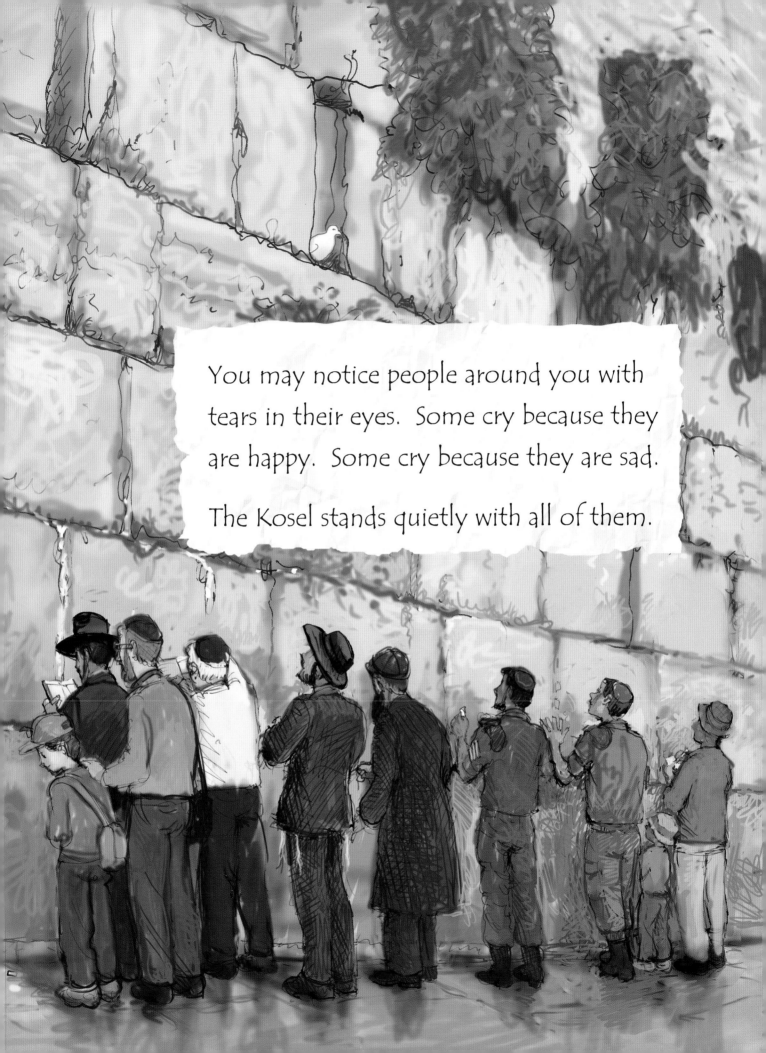

You may notice people around you with tears in their eyes. Some cry because they are happy. Some cry because they are sad.

The Kosel stands quietly with all of them.

High up, nearer to the sky, living things make their homes in the shelter of the Kosel. Plants grow between the stones. Birds, gray and white doves, nest in the little hollows where some of the stone has broken away. It seems like those birds are watching the people below... watching and waiting.

Maybe today, the time for waiting will end at last. Maybe today, someone will say that one tefillah – do that one kindness – that will finally bring peace and happiness to the world. Maybe you will be the one.

From high above, the doves might be the first to see it. Imagine them puffing up their feathers, spreading their wings to swoop down and watch as we sing and dance with joy.

Perhaps they will circle above our heads, celebrating with a dance of their own, in the blue, blue sky above the Wall.

But for now, we will keep asking for Moshiach to come. We will stand together, doing what we can to help one another.

The Kosel has waited for a very long time now.
We are waiting, too. We are waiting by the Wall.

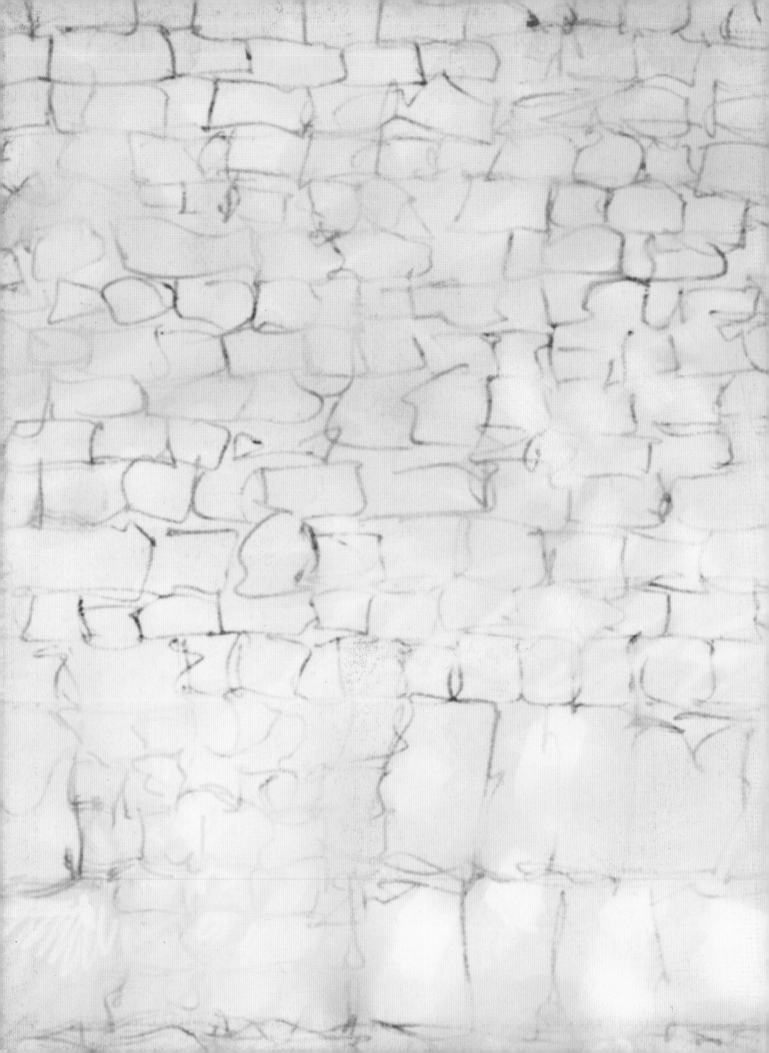